Garden of Stars

by Dwaine Spieker

The author is grateful to the editors of the following publications in which some of these poems first appeared: *Plainsongs, Nebraska Poets Calendar, Nebraska Life, Omaha World-Herald, Plain Song Review*, and *Platte Valley Review*.

"My Father at Twenty-Nine" and "*In Medias Res*" are reprinted from *Prairie Schooner,* Volume 80, Number 1 (Spring 2006) by permission of the University of Nebraska Press.

ISBN for All Along Press hardback edition: 978-0-615-34576-5

ISBN for this Lulu paperback edition: 978-0-557-58345-4

– for Mollie

List of Titles

Prologue

Trees in Winter

These are the old farmers
who have taken off their caps
and sit at the kitchen table
with their wives, the gardens.

With so little to do with their hands
until spring, there is little to say.

I

In Medias Res

The cardinal landed
and said:

There is no beginning,
only the point at which
you began to pay attention.

At Some Point in the Past

The songs the stars used to sing
split with the light they still have,

rained onto skies of grass,
rained onto night-colored insects.

The light was lesser for it,
and days now darken as the songs

cricket, cricket to get back.

A Miniature Tea Set

Tonight the stars are cups and saucers
on the knick-knack shelf of the heavens,
a set of miniature china service
arranged around the teapot of the moon,
each setpiece dusty from generations
of resting just like this, out of reach,
too delicate and fragile for the grandchildren.

Center Pivot

All night, a mile off,
a Chevy 454
rams a piston of sound
through every last
cricket-cylinder
of the fields. Above
and around it,
as cool and quiet
as sprinklers,
walk the stars.

Sunrise, 5:14

There is dew this morning on the tractor seat.

In the grass an old harrow itches
with rust, near the base of a power pole

and a Rural Electric meter, its glass bowl
still fogged with yesterday's humidity.

No air conditioners. The day's wind
hasn't switched on yet.

To the east, a young charolais
lifts its head, lumbers to the feed bunk.

There is day, before the first human wakes up.

Housecat

Look. He licks himself to sleep
there on the sill, unaware
if outside it is hot or cold,
if beyond the limits of his vision
there is any world.
Forgivable, in a feline,
to forget such trifles.
He rules this tiny house so well,
brings all corners under his control,
we must forgive him if,
having long ago conquered the couch
and the dining room table,
he feels he rules over all.

Snowblower

There is no mystery in this,
when a frigid Briggs & Stratton
arcs all that accumulated silence
over an azure cirrus

of exhaust. No mystery,
but also no riddle:
from a discotheque of friction
and the rattle of loose panels

comes intolerance for chaos,
and a single semi-circle
of industrial snowfall,
which is not unbeautiful—

Rain Gauge

Mounted on a fencepost out in back
is our little way of knowing things,
a clear cylinder of thin glass
six inches tall
(because it rarely rains more than that).

When the neighbors up the road
say they got a half-inch more than we did,
we are glad for them, but return home
to double-check we read right what ours said,
fairly sure our gauge is more accurate.

Old Irish Widow

Forecasted like a summer storm,
Great Aunt Velda drove out for visits
in her Grand Marquis the size and shape
of a thunderhead. Her denim skirts
reminded me of rain on the horizon,
and how she laughed and what she laughed at
reminded me of hail. Like wind, she never
said hello or goodbye—she simply arrived
and was herself, picking at the coffee cake
my mother baked for her.
                    Sometimes when she'd gone
we'd had an inch or more of good, hard rain.
Other times, all the crops were beaten to sticks
and my mother was crying.

Old Eagles

Old Eagles perch at Nestled Inn,
  Clipped wings rest, holding beer:
They wore the black the Eagles wore
  For ball, back yesteryear.

Chip winged the shot that snatched the crown
  The year he won All-State:
The ball sailed smooth, then dropped, then fell—
  You'd swear it looked like fate.

To watch him play was poetry:
  This Eagle read in flight.
He mused in motion offense
  Though he could barely write.

Now Mitch, his dad, beside him sits:
  These Eagles have gone bald.
Tonight they'll watch Chip's son suit up,
  And Chick can shoot that ball.

As Chip lands at the game tonight,
  Drunk, past a sign he'll sail:
"Eagle Basketball is Life:
  The Rest is Just Details."

Recess

Today the afternoon stretches out
like a playground, and the world

has been let out of class: hills
leapfrogging each other to the horizon,

clouds doing cartwheels and somersaults,
tall grass riding the swings,

the river sparkling up the monkeybars,

and even the adult sun joins in,
hopscotching along.

Yet through it all cuts the highway,
cool and sullen as an eighth-grader,

wishing to be somewhere else, far from here.

North of Schuyler, Nebraska

The ocean of corn has drowned another barn
and tossed it on a beach of thistles.

Retriever

It's been snowing all day
and my dog is sprawled on the living room carpet,
sleeping the simpering way big dogs sleep
when they sleep hard. Right now

he is swimming the lake of his inner life,
paws twitching with joy as he parts the dark water,
retrieving the fallen drake of a dream
in the mouth of his mind.

But in that dream he turns around
to bring it back to me, and sees
I am not there. He jolts awake and over to me
with that abandoned look on his face:

How could you do such a thing?
He licks my hand as if he's misbehaved.

Coyotes

Coyotes are completely free
of complaint, of self-pity.

Those midnight yelps are calls
of perfect contentment.

Scavengers, they are always happy
with whatever happens along,

and do not distinguish live flesh
from carrion.

They roam their whole lives
unlimited by leash or kennel.

They can digest anything,
no matter how maggoty,

and are just as happy to starve.

Laundry Chute

Most old houses have a dark, silent shaft
that falls like an upside-down chimney
through the walls. With an easily forgotten
slip and dismissal, down it go family things
too wrinkled or embarrassing to bring up
in polite conversation. Although it has saved
everyone who lives there (and even some visitors)
countless trips down the creaky steps
of awkward silence, there's usually one person
who disappears downstairs every day
to empty the hamper and sort what has fallen
by color and fabric, who from decades of practice
is such an expert at cleaning things up
and smoothing them out, hardly anyone notices.

In October

Who can blame the garden
for having pulled a quilt of frost
down from the closet, for curling up
and nodding off, even before
his work was really done for the year?

Between All Souls and Thanksgiving

Once again this year,
the garden of summer has gotten away from us,
overgrown with the weeds of our inattention.

Now the rusty mower of November
is cutting everything off clean.
Next year, we promise ourselves,
next year we'll stay on top of things.

II

After a Spring Snowstorm

1. *Canada Geese*

A flock of Canada geese,
reined like a team of horses
to the wagon of spring,
gallops north, two hundred strong.

Watch: the wooden spokes
on the wheels of March
are turning so fast
they seem to spin backwards.

2. *Robins*

Having flitted up
out of distant history,
they gather here at
the birdbath of the present

to wet their feathers and drink.

3. *Blue Spruce*

As the big band of spring
tunes its horns and trombones,
he's got robins in his eyes
and, in one side of his mouth,
a peppermint of snow. Once again
it's 1946, the war is over, and he too
is in the mood, looking around
for someone evergreen, someone
who after all these winters
still really knows how to swing.

4. *Tulips*

The tulips have unfolded their knives
and whittle away at the snow.
Meanwhile they tell the same old stories
as ever, but with fresh details.

5. *Crocuses*

Out at the end of our sidewalk
are the artesian wells of our yard,
where spring has tapped the aquifer
through a crack in the earth's strata
and captured the natural, upward
bubbling of color. As you stand there
in early April, it seems the whole
world runneth over, cool and clear,
with delicate petals. And you'd swear
yes, things could flow on like this forever.

III

January

– in memory of my grandfather

When he died snow blew for three days
and his driveway drifted closed
with our sorrow. After the wake
a few of the cousins from Omaha
went to his workshop to weep: Soon cold,
they ran back inside for chili
and left the walk-in door wide open.

Next morning sun showed us what happened:
Wind, as always, found everything
and left a fine shimmer of snow,
light as a soul, on each of his tools.

Window Open, January

Over the melting ice and snow,
the sound of a car being started:
someone is turning spring's cold engine
over and over with the ignition
of a January thaw. If he succeeds
and the motor engages, for one day at least,
the vehicle will run as well
as if it were April, and many of us
will hop in and go for a long drive
down the road of our hopes for the year.

Frost

Although a thaw had blurred his vision,
Winter once again has donned
his bifocals of cold, and is looking hard
at every grain and blade of the world.

Driving Back to David City, Nebraska, After a Postseason Basketball Game

– for Mollie

We drive south out of Schuyler
in a long line of Aquinas High fans
sulking homeward after the subdistrict

final. To me it feels like a funeral
procession, slow and lighted, weeping
down Highway 15 toward home,

baseball season, and spring. Amid them all
we ride in my red Thunderbird,
radio at a careful, low level. No one

wants to get home, to tell a mirror
of another season spent and what it cost.
So. I reach over to hold your hand.

In this February darkness,
I let all the others talk of loss.

Penny

The full moon is copper-colored,
a shiny penny on the dark sidewalk
of the sky. It's not worth much
by itself, but I think I'll add it to
the change jar of small things
I'm happy about this morning.
It all adds up.

Coffee Shop

Already at five a.m. the coffee shop is lit up
like an old television, its bay window to Main Street
a staticy screen, a big silver donut rack
bringing in the signal. But this time of day
is too early for drama, so our small-town station
is broadcasting reruns: black-and-white or technicolor
comedies and westerns. Bang gently a few times
on one side of the morning, and what do you know,
there's Burt Lancaster, rehearsing weather and markets
with Jackie Gleason and Ward Cleaver, Andy Griffith
and the Lone Ranger. You can catch each of these men
starring all day long in a series of his own
somewhere in town, on a farm or a highway, in a factory,
lumberyard, or classroom. Yet for now they're together
on the same channel, humming a single theme song
with the old cast of familiars, while strong coffee
adjusts the vertical hold on their working lives.
Through the mono speaker of the shop's screen door
ring out the silver six-shooters of their laughter.

John Deere

After his heart blew up
like an under-oiled engine,
they had to tow him to town.

Now he's been overhauled
and painted up, so every day
down to the coffee shop
then around on errands
for his wife, he parades.

Two Weeks to Summer Vacation

On the school lawn, under a linden,
a robin dangles a nightcrawler
from its beak, then exactly as
a fisherman cinches a worm up
onto a hook, the robin loops it over
and over in its beak, and then
as if to cast itself
into the warm pond of a May afternoon,
it winds up, flicks
the tight wrist of its body, and is gone.

Daughter

When you were born,
someone clicked on
my heart's quiet radio,
and day and night since
it's been playing good songs.

The Robin

stitches the cloth
of sunlight.

In the yellow needle
of its beak,

the gold thread
of song.

How rich the tunic
of spring!

Cottonwood

As seed I weighed nothing:
mistaken for spring snow,
left to my own auspices
deep in the sandhills.

Mistake me not, though,
for sentimental: out here
the wind is a mad god,
the sun unmusical,

my stem scratched smooth
by the asses of unconcerned cattle.

Alone I discovered
my supramental labor:
yearly to give flight
to a thousand self-vessels,

to find, to ramify,
to give whatever I can
root out of this sand
hue, shape, height.

Lines for my Father

Dad, like a scratched-up jackknife,
may your blade stay silver
and stainless enough to lance
and drain a calf's abscess;

and later, after a bath
from a hydrant, be clean
and steel enough to peel the skin

off an apple, keeping your tip
abrupt enough to be dropped
on a wooden floor and stick
straight up.

And later yet, when your blade folds back
to your handle
for good,

may I hold you, my lockblade,
always warm in my pocket.

Memorial Day Flyover

Like the scores of American flags
that line the cemetery drives,
we throw one-handed shadows
over our eyes, and like silk flowers
decorating a shoulder-high headstone,
our blankets, lawn chairs, and strollers
wreathe the temporary podium
where, over a crackling microphone,
speakers have just read the Gettysburg Address,
"In Flanders Fields," and several
non-sectarian prayers. Beyond us, on a knoll,
the high-school band, exact as a salute
and fresh off "America the Beautiful,"
sparkles like a chest of medals.

Then, on schedule, the jets rip past,
and in their afterburn we clap, gather things,
and scatter toward the cemetery gates.
Even the band goes suddenly cacophonous
and non-sectarian. Although a few of us
linger, looking for relatives' graves,
we've come and gone so fast that, to the dead,
we must resemble a scheduled flyover
as we flatten grass, brush branches,
and snap stems of peonies grown plush.

Old Cow

Late into morning, a southwest wind
tongues the salt-lick of humidity,
scratches her neck on a cottonwood's bark,
and grazes her way out to pasture.

Between now and nightfall, as meadowlarks
twitter like ripples of sunlit tankwater,
she'll swish her tail along the hills,
lumbering yet light in her oblivion.

Hummingbird

Only if life
    calms at center

can its periphery
    be absolute flutter.

Summer 1990

When Kansas City played on the West Coast,
I slept with my radio.

I'd listen long enough
to hear the middle relievers called in

and the scores arrive from all the East-Coast contests
before I flew out to short center.

Sometimes I'd wake long after the game had ended
and the station had gone off the air

to find myself tuned to the contests of crickets
and the radio static of stars.

Quonset

A semi-cylinder of tin
    With a smooth cement floor,
Where my father worked iron
    And parked tractors.

Sparrows nested in the apex.
    Near the door, a red welder.
Dust and gnarled feed sacks
    Gathered in the corners.

Sweeping the floor clean
    Was my job every summer.
Machinery gone, the sparrows' songs
    (Like the music of the spheres)

Sweetened as they echoed off tin
    And concrete. It was there
I learned even I too could sing
    If I spoke upward.

My Father at Twenty-Nine

In the denim of dawn,
he sat at his end of the kitchen table
to buckle his workboots.

Leaning forward,
his back was a pasture of muscle
as the sun broke over it.

Already, this early,
he carried the sky.

Ward Farm

If someday I have left this smog,
away from this advancing city
where self-suspicion taxes all my earnings;
if ever I have left this falsewood desk
where I stamp-sign my name to paper sins;
if I should ever quit this high-rise office,

I shall return to that far-off farm,
where shelterbelts of pines and maples
rim the south field,
where bluejays do not care what my name is,
where purple silks sit moistly on the cornstalks
no matter what I do or say or am.

There I shall lie down among the nodding brome
along a loosening barbed-wire fence,
forget that I was ever I or someone's friend or son,
turn to the earth, be gone.

Country Cemetery

No water for a hundred miles
in any direction, yet this afternoon
the dead have pulled their oars in,

have set stone sails out to the breeze,
and sit back in their skiffs, knitting
or trying to find luck with the fish.

At least for now they seem content
to drift on this same sea of hills,
this easy swell of pastures and cornfields,

forever and ever, weaving sweaters
of blue spruce and fountain grass,
netting bouquets every so often.

Boy on a Bicycle

With the same sound a cicada makes
fluttering against a window screen,
a boy rides by on his bicycle.

He's clothes-pinned a playing card
to the bike's frame, so that the spokes
brush against it and sound like a motor.

It's too soon yet, but in a short while
the boy will molt that bike the same way
a cicada abandons its shell, the fluttering

gone with the long light of August,
the bike still warm with the boy's form
long after he motors into the world.

To My Son, Having Found his Hands

Turning them over and over again
before your eyes, you pause, consider
the tip of your left index finger,
and learn how far it can extend.
Then, concentrating hard, you draw them in
like two unnested, flightless birds
you cannot hold for their flutter
and cannot release for fascination.

Already, aged only half a year,
you know yourself from fingertip to wrist.
I pray your hand-examination never ends.
Gifts from your great-grandfather,
they are yours to do with as you wish,
yours for good, yours over and over again.

A Bright and Breezy Afternoon

I have left town behind me
like a crowded beach

and waded out into the grass.
It laps at my legs.

Out here I am a sundial
and weathervane. I can sense

sixty-four compass points
on a map of the soul.

I am a constellation:
star-cornered,

lost in the daylight that fills me.

Geometry Teacher

It had to hurt her infinitely
to watch us fumble with our compasses
in fourth-hour geometry.
She taught us absolutes, the pure forms,
a perfect Platonist,
but we were sophomores, askew in body
and mind: we spiked our hair.

God, she must have suffered
whenever I drew my circles freehand,
as if pure shape meant nothing,
did my assignment too quickly, in pen,
and tore it gruffly from a spiral.
Even now, form greets me hard.

But she preserved for years the pure,
the equilateral, the square,
and so to her, high praise,
for all her years of hearkening to perfect form,
for tolerance of sophomores,
for holding Shape and Student parallel
and narrowing the infinity between.

In the Rocking Chair with my Son, 5:45 a.m.

The leather chair rocks back and forth;
  You snore your baby snore.
The living room is still and dark;
  The cat sits by the door.

The crickets sing their old, old tunes;
  The stars click off like lights.
We're up but not quite risen,
  This last hour of the night.

My son, you'll be an early riser,
  I sense, just like your father.
For eighteen months we've rocked like this,
  Here, as mornings gathered.

But dawn allows for back-and-forth
  And paradoxes gleaming:
You are both up and fast asleep,
  I am awake and dreaming.

Jars of Tomatoes

Just out of the boiling water,
they are as warm as hearts
and seem to glow—sealed inside
is the growth of a whole summer.

Within their glass containers,
they'll hold onto summer through fall
to help make our winter soups
Valentine-colored. And here, Love,

I give you my own heart, sealed
just for you, like a jar of tomatoes.
It's fragile but full of summer,
so warm for you that it glows.

Traveler

A giant moth, the size
of my palm, is gripping
the south side of our house
with the fingers of fall,

its graying knuckles
holding the cracked handle
of its small, worn
suitcase of world.

Somewhere deep inside
its worn trenchcoat
a pocketwatch ticks,
a small clock of light

that the traveler checks
in the emptying station
of these September days.
He's right on schedule.

Yellow Maple

Back in the middle of October,
autumn reached up into the lampshade
of this tree and, with a click of frost,
turned the bulb on. Now the season,
under the soft light of falling leaves,
leans back in its old recliner, beginning
a long novel of wind and gray weather.

Cornfield

Refusing to turn on the furnace
until November,

she has shawled herself in the wool
of withered tassels

and sits spooning a sunset,
her steaming tea.

Grandmother

November again, and our burning bush
is doing chores, a red handkerchief
on its head, tight across the scalp
and tied snug in back, one corner
flagging over gathered, bobbed hair,
perfect, exactly how my grandmother
scarfed herself when she fed chickens.

November, and I can see her again
inside her coop's wicker-wire yard,
carrying grain to the crowding hens
with an old coffee can. The same deep red
perfection marks this bush's labor
as it pours out the grain of autumn
into the long metal trough of winter.

The Gardener in Winter

Inside unwillingly, the gardener
from dead wood grows living fire.
Then his hands sleep. Outside, the hoar-air
imitates stars.

It's come again to this: his harvest
canned and bagged and cellared,
his fire is the imitation flower
he will tend all winter,

the cold an imitation rain,
rain that softens the flower.
There is a time to plant, a time
to uproot the plant,

and this time too, when the gardener
retreats into his fruit.

The Gardener in Winter

Epilogue

Camping in October

This forest clearing
is a dark flower,

a campfire the stamen
around which I hover,

collecting light like pollen
in the garden of stars.

Acknowledgements

Garden of Stars was first published in a hardback, letterpress edition of 200 copies by Elysia Mann of All Along Press in St. Louis, MO in 2009 and 2010. No subsequent edition of this book, especially a computer-generated paperback version, can suggest the inimitable handiwork of the first edition. The author is grateful to Elysia for her accuracy and artistry throughout this project.

The author is also tremendously grateful to his wife, Mollie, for initiating the project. It was time.

About the Author

Dwaine Spieker grew up on a farm at the eastern edge of the Nebraska Sandhills before attending the University of Nebraska at Kearney and the University of Nebraska-Lincoln. He now teaches high-school and college English in Wayne, Nebraska, where he lives with his wife, Mollie, and three children.

Fourteen years in the making, this is his first book.